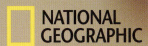

Machines in Sports

USING SIMPLE MACHINES

Caroline Snow

PICTURE CREDITS
Cover: men playing baseball in Santa Fe, New Mexico © Marc Romanelli/Image Bank/Getty Images; man climbing rock, Photodisc; man riding mountain bike, Image 100 Ltd.

page 1 © Tom & Dee Ann McCarthy/Corbis/Tranz; page 4 (bottom left), Corbis; page 4 (bottom right), Photodisc; page 5 (top) © Duomo/Corbis/Tranz; page 5 (bottom left) © Corbis/Tranz; page 5 (bottom right), Corbis; page 6 © Michael Kim/Corbis/Tranz; page 7 (left) © Museum of the City of New York/Corbis/Tranz; page 7 (right), image 100 Ltd; page 8 © Pete Saloutos/Corbis/Tranz; page 9, Photodisc; page 11 © Jeff Kowalsky/AFP; page 12 © Paul A. Souders/Corbis/Tranz; page 13 © LWA-Dann Tardif/Corbis/Tranz; page 14 © Tom Raymond/Stone/Getty Images; page 15 © Macmillan Publishers New Zealand; page 21, © Photodisc; page 29, Corbis.

Illustrations: pages 10–18 by Andrew Aguilar; pages 23–26 by Pat Kermode.

Produced through the worldwide resources of the National Geographic Society, John M. Fahey, Jr., President and Chief Executive Officer; Gilbert M. Grosvenor, Chairman of the Board; Nina D. Hoffman, Executive Vice President and President, Books and Education Publishing Group.

PREPARED BY NATIONAL GEOGRAPHIC SCHOOL PUBLISHING
Ericka Markman, Senior Vice President and President, Children's Books and Education Publishing Group; Steve Mico, Vice President and Editorial Director; Marianne Hiland, Executive Editor; Richard Easby, Editorial Manager; Jim Hiscott, Design Manager; Kristin Hanneman, Illustrations Manager; Matt Wascavage, Manager of Publishing Services; Sean Philpotts, Production Manager.

EDITORIAL MANAGEMENT
Morrison BookWorks, LLC

PROGRAM CONSULTANTS
Dr. Shirley V. Dickson, Program Director, Literacy, Education Commission of the States; James A. Shymansky, E. Desmond Lee Professor of Science Education, University of Missouri-St. Louis.

National Geographic Theme Sets program developed by Macmillan Education Australia, Pty Limited.

Published by the National Geographic Society
1145 17th Street, N.W.
Washington, D.C. 20036-4688

ISBN: 978-0-7922-4755-5
ISBN: 0-7922-4755-8

Printed in Hong Kong.

2011 2010 2009 2008
4 5 6 7 8 9 10 11 12 13 14 15

Contents

Using Simple Machines

When you hear the word *machine*, what is the first thing that comes to your mind? Perhaps you think of a dishwasher or a vacuum cleaner. These are both machines, but a broom and a knife are also machines. Basically, a machine is any kind of device that helps you do something more easily. People use simple machines every day—at home, in sports, on construction sites, and in health care.

 ## Key Concepts..

1. Machines use force to help people do work.
2. There are six simple machines.
3. Compound machines use two or more simple machines operating together.

Where Machines Are Found

In the Home

Simple machines help people with many different tasks in the home.

In Sports

Simple machines are a part of many types of sports equipment.

In this book you will learn about simple machines used in sports, such as this bat.

In Construction

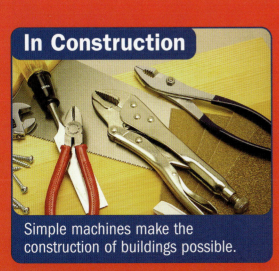

Simple machines make the construction of buildings possible.

In Health

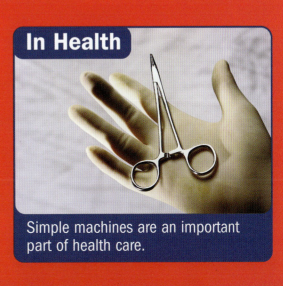

Simple machines are an important part of health care.

Machines

in Sports

Think of all the sports you have played or watched. What sports can you think of that involve machines? People who race cars use machines. People also use machines when they row or sail. In-line skates and bikes are machines, too. But what about a baseball bat or a tennis racket? These things are also machines that people use in sports.

Some machines used in sports have many moving parts, such as bicycles and sailboats. Some machines run on fuel, such as race cars and jet boats. Some machines, such as bats and rackets, do not run on fuel and do not have moving parts. All these machines do one thing, though. They make the actions people do in sports easier.

A race car is a machine with many moving parts.

Machines – Past and Present

People use many machines when they play sports. Many of these machines are based on tools from long ago. For example, one important machine long ago was the **wheel and axle**. The wheel and axle helped people move from place to place. One of the early wheel and axle machines people used was the bicycle. Bicycles were also used in sports. People raced each other on bicycles and still do today. There are many different sports that use wheels and axles.

Bicycles from long ago look different from modern bicycles.

Bicycles are used in many sporting events.

Force and Work

To understand how machines operate, you first need to understand **force** and work. Force is something that makes an object move, stop, or change. Whenever you play sports, you use force. You use force when you kick a ball because you make it move. You use force when you catch a ball because you make it stop. You use force when you swim because you make your body move through the water.

> **force**
> something that moves, changes, or stops an object

These swimmers are using force as they move through the water.

Did you know that when you play sports you are doing **work**? In science, work is the result of force moving, stopping, or changing an object. So every time you use force on an object to cause it to move in some way, you are doing work. Even when you are playing, you can be doing work. For example, you work when you jump rope. The force from your arms causes the rope to move.

work
the result of force moving, stopping, or changing an object

Machines make the work you do easier. If you tried to paddle a kayak with just your hands, it would not move very fast. A paddle helps you move the kayak. The paddle allows you to exert more force on the water.

machines
tools or other devices that help people do work

This kayaker is doing work. The paddles make his work easier.

The Six Simple Machines

There are six **simple machines**. Simple machines are designed to change how forces act.

simple machines
devices that change how forces act

The Wedge

A **wedge** is an object with one or more sloping sides. A wedge may end in a sharp edge or point. People use wedges to cut or split objects.

Arrowheads used in archery are examples of wedges. The pointed shape of an arrowhead helps the arrow pierce its target. The arrowhead splits the target as it pierces it.

Wedge

Sloping surface

Movement

Movement

Force

Sloping surface

Movement

Movement

Force

This arrowhead is a wedge.

The Lever

A **lever** is a straight bar or rod. A lever turns or swivels on a fixed point called a **fulcrum**. People use levers to lift things. The thing a lever lifts is called a **load**. The end of the bar that pushes the load is called the load arm. The end of the bar where force is applied is called the force arm. A lever can reduce the force needed to lift a load.

When you row a boat, you use an oar to move the boat through the water. The oar is a type of lever. You apply force to one end of the oar. This force pushes the other end of the oar against the water. This moves the boat along.

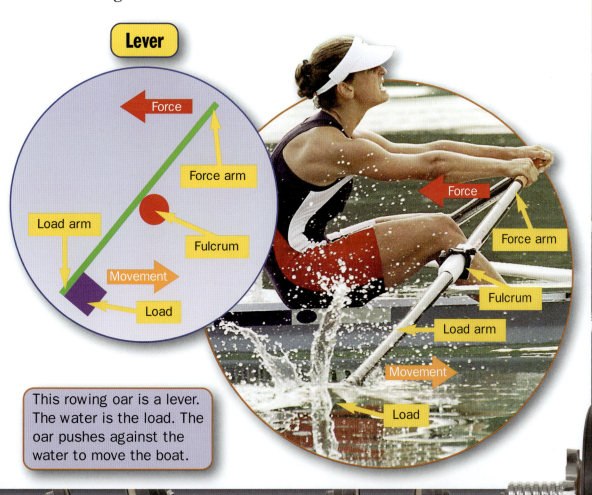

Lever

Force

Force arm

Load arm

Fulcrum

Movement

Load

Force

Force arm

Fulcrum

Load arm

Movement

Load

This rowing oar is a lever. The water is the load. The oar pushes against the water to move the boat.

The Inclined Plane

An **inclined plane** is a flat, slanted surface with a high end and a low end. A ramp is an example of an inclined plane. People use ramps to move loads up and down. It usually takes less force to use a ramp than to lift a load straight up.

Skateboarders use ramps. Going down ramps allows them to build up the speed they need to do tricks.

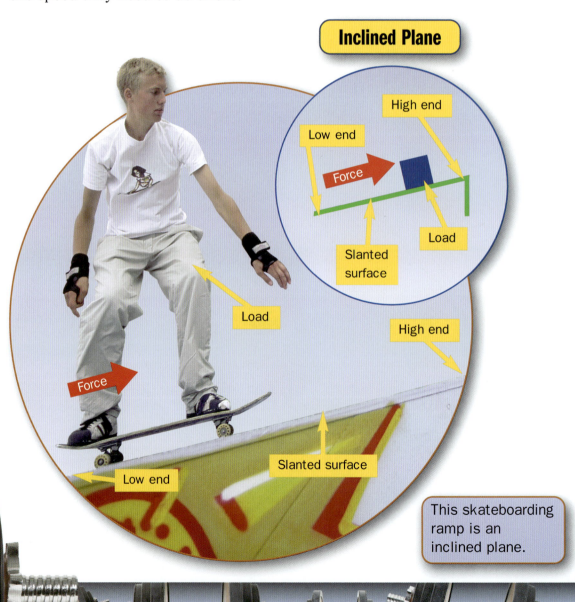

Inclined Plane

High end

Low end

Force

Slanted surface

Load

Load

High end

Force

Slanted surface

Low end

This skateboarding ramp is an inclined plane.

The Screw

A **screw** is a simple machine that is often used to fasten objects together. It is made up of a pole with a sloped ridge that spirals around it. This ridge is called the **thread**. When a screw is turned, its thread winds into the object that is at the tip of the screw. The more the screw is turned, the deeper it moves in. A screw can go through two objects to hold them together. To remove a screw, it is turned in the opposite direction. It can't be pulled straight out without damaging the screw or the object.

Screws are useful in sports because they are strong. They can be used to hold the parts of sports equipment together. The weights on some weightlifting equipment are held in place by a screw.

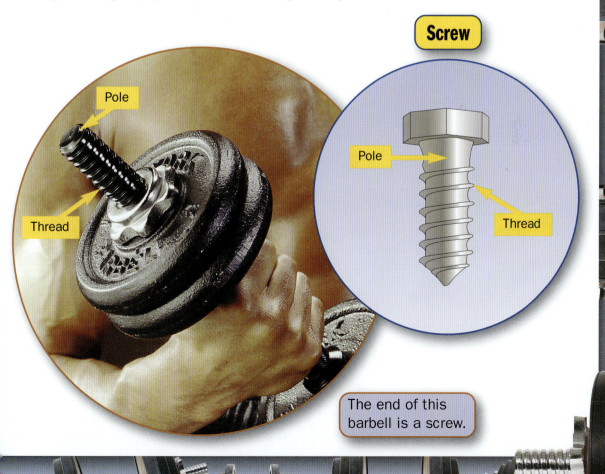

Screw

Pole

Thread

Pole

Thread

The end of this barbell is a screw.

The Wheel and Axle

Another kind of simple machine is the wheel and axle. This machine has a wheel that turns on a pole. The pole is called an axle. The larger wheel and the smaller axle are joined and turn together. So turning the larger wheel makes the smaller axle turn more slowly but with a stronger force. Or, turning the smaller axle makes the larger wheel turn faster but with less force.

A race car driver turns the steering wheel to change the direction of the car. The steering wheel uses a wheel and axle machine. Turning the wheel makes the smaller axle turn more slowly but with more force. The turning axle moves other parts of the car that turn the wheels to change the car's direction.

Wheel and Axle

Force

Movement

Wheel

Axle

Force

Movement

Wheel

Axle

A steering wheel uses a wheel and axle machine.

The Pulley

A simple **pulley** is a wheel with a grooved rim. A rope in the groove wraps around the wheel. One end is attached to a load. People pull on the other end to move the load. With a single pulley, the weight of the load and the force needed to move it are equal. A single pulley allows you to pull in one direction to move a load in the opposite direction.

Some weights machines use pulleys. People pull on a rope that wraps around the wheel and connects to the weights. The pulley lets people pull in different directions, using different muscles, to lift the weights.

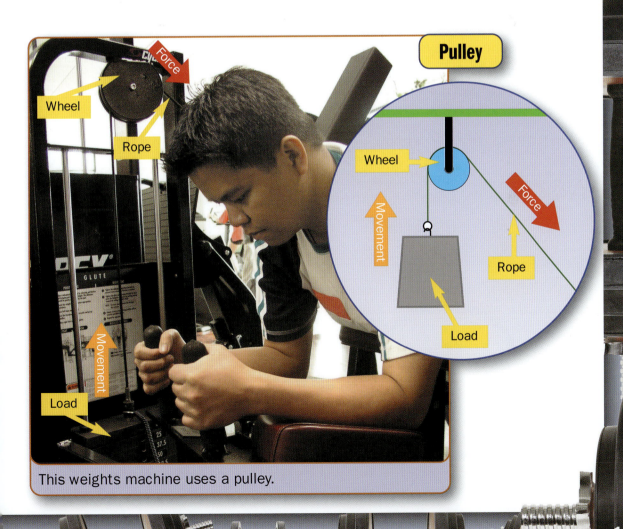

This weights machine uses a pulley.

Working with Machines in Sports

Machines used in sports can be both simple and **compound machines**. Compound machines are made up of two or more simple machines put together.

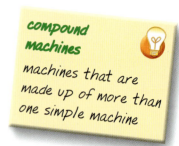

compound machines

machines that are made up of more than one simple machine

Bicycle

A bicycle is a compound machine made up of many simple machines. The pedals are part of a wheel and axle machine. They connect to a toothed wheel called a sprocket. A chain loops around the sprocket and a set of toothed pulleys, or **gears**. These gears are connected to the axle of the back wheel. When you turn the pedals, they turn the sprocket. The sprocket pulls the chain, which turns the gears. The gears turn the axle, turning the back wheel.

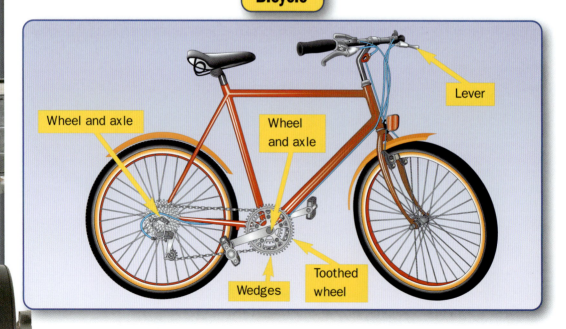

Bicycle

Lever

Wheel and axle

Wheel and axle

Wedges

Toothed wheel

Sailboat

A sailboat is a compound machine. A sailboat uses a lever to change direction. The lever is made up of a tiller that is joined to a rudder. The bow of a sailboat is a wedge. It pushes water aside as the boat moves through the water. A sailboat also uses pulleys. A rope called a mainsheet is threaded through a pulley and attached to the sail. People control the sail by pulling on or releasing the mainsheet. The mainsheet moves easily through the pulley.

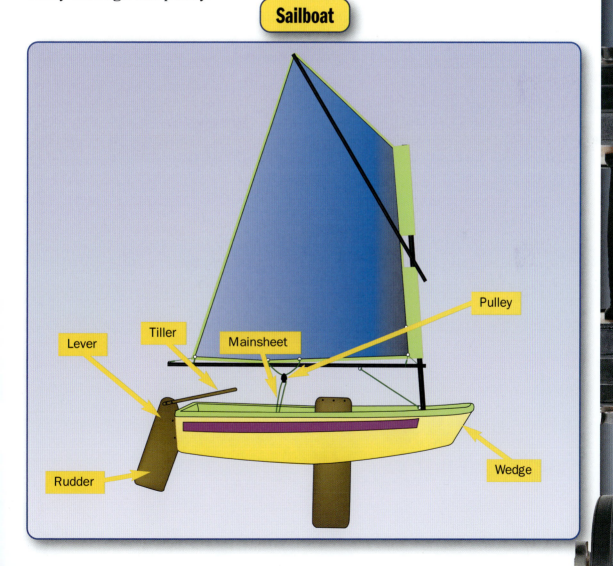

Sailboat

Lever

Tiller

Mainsheet

Pulley

Rudder

Wedge

Pitching Machine

A pitching machine is a compound machine. Baseball and softball players use pitching machines. The machine throws balls to them, so they can practice hitting. Pitching machines such as the one shown here have two wheels. Motors turn the axles, and the axles turn the wheels. The balls roll into the machine down an inclined plane. The spinning wheels throw the balls forward. The faster the wheels are turning, the faster the pitch.

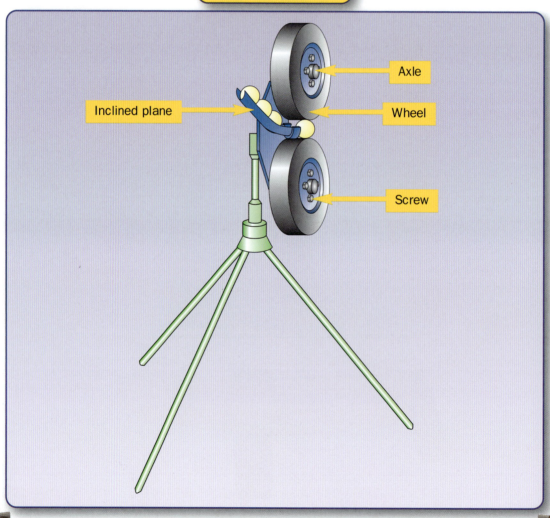

Pitching Machine

Inclined plane

Axle

Wheel

Screw

Think About the **Key Concepts**

Think about what you read. Think about the pictures and diagrams. Use these to answer the questions. Share what you think with others.

1. What are three things that force can do to an object? Give an example of each.

2. In science, what is the connection between force and work?

3. Name the six simple machines. Explain how each one can help people work.

4. Give two examples of compound machines. Explain how they help people work.

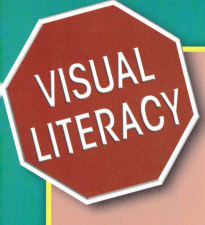

Labeled Photograph

Photographs show you real-life examples of ideas discussed in books or articles.

A **labeled photograph** provides extra information. The labels show you the important parts of the photograph you should be looking at.

Look back at the labeled photographs on pages 11–15. These are labeled examples of simple machines used in sports. The labeled photograph on page 21 is an example of a compound machine used in sports: a fishing rod.

How to Read a Labeled Photograph

1. Read the title.

The title tells you the subject, or what the photograph is about.

2. Read the labels and caption.

Labels and captions tell you about the subject and its parts.

3. Study the photograph.

Connect the information in the photograph to what you have read in the text.

Fishing Rod

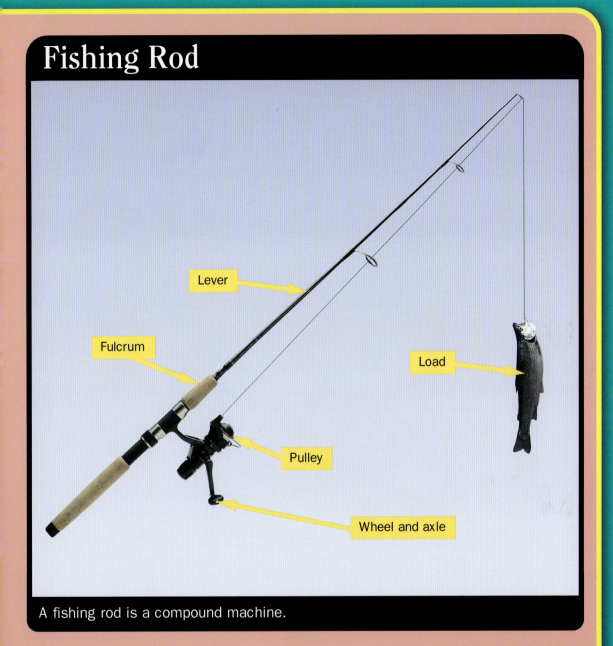

Lever

Fulcrum

Load

Pulley

Wheel and axle

A fishing rod is a compound machine.

What Can You See?

Read the photograph by following the steps on page 20. Now look back at the diagrams of compound machines on pages 16–18. Can you draw a basic diagram showing the simple machines in a fishing rod?

How-to Books

The purpose of **how-to books** is to give directions. How-to books take many forms.

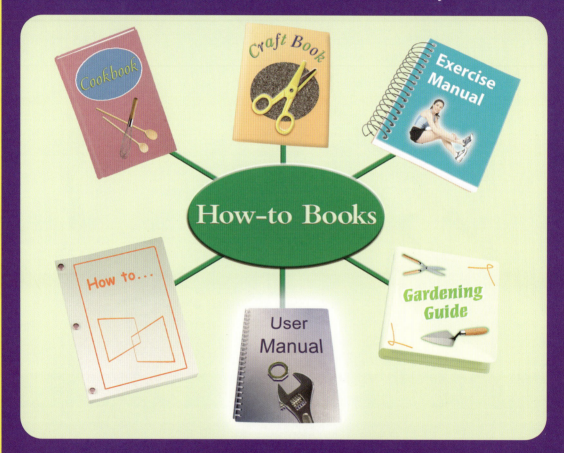

You use different how-to books to find out how to do different things. If you want to know how to use a machine, you read a **user manual**. User manuals come with machines when you buy them.

User manuals give you all the information you need to know before you use a machine. They tell you how to operate the machine. They also tell you how to care for the machine and how to use it safely.

Bicycle User Manual

Congratulations on buying a new bicycle. Inside this user manual, you will find directions on using your bicycle. You will also learn how to clean and care for it. Follow these instructions, and you will get many years of use from your bicycle.

The **title** tells you which machine the user manual is for.

Parts of the Bicycle

Subheads break the information into easy-to-find sections.

1. seat
2. handlebar
3. gear lever
4. brake and gear control cables
5. front brake
6. tire
7. spokes
8. chain wheel
9. axle
10. chain
11. crank
12. pedal

Labels show the parts of the machine.

Figure A

Before You Ride

Important information is presented in bulleted lists so it is easy to find and read.

Safety Check

Before you ride your bicycle, you should always do a safety check.

- Check that the front and rear brakes are working.
- Make sure the tires are not flat. They should be firm when squeezed.
- Check that the pedals are fixed tightly to the cranks.
- Make sure the chain is oiled and clean.

Checking the Seat Height

Check that the bicycle seat height is right for you.

- Sit on the bicycle with one pedal at its lowest point.
- Place the ball of your foot on the pedal. If the seat is at the best height, your leg will be slightly bent (Figure B).

You may need to change the seat height.

- Use a wrench to loosen the nut at the back of the seat.
- Raise or lower the seat to the right height.
- Tighten the nut with the wrench.

Figure B

Wearing a Helmet

You should always wear a helmet when riding a bicycle (Figure C).

- Your helmet must meet safety standards.
- Your helmet should fit firmly on your head.
- Your helmet must be strapped on when you are riding your bicycle.

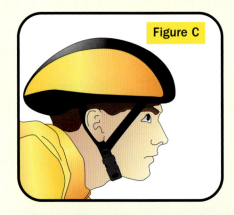

Figure C

Riding the Bicycle

Riding Safely

- Use hand signals to show that you are about to turn a corner. The man in the picture is signaling that he will turn left (Figure D).

- Unless signaling, always keep both hands on the handlebars. Keep your feet on the pedals.

- Keep the brakes on when riding downhill.

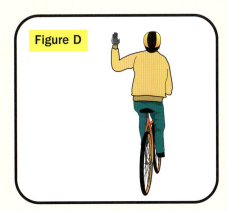

Figure D

Changing Gears

Your bicycle has different gears. Lower gears make pedaling easier, but you will move slower. Higher gears make pedaling harder, but you will move faster.

- Change gears by shifting the gear lever on the handlebar (Figure E).

- Keep pedaling as you change gears.

- Use lower gears for riding uphill.

- Use higher gears for riding downhill or on a flat road.

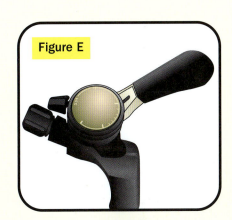

Figure E

Turning Corners

- Brake lightly when you are coming up to the corner.

- Do not pedal.

- Lean your body inward slightly as you go around the corner.

- Never turn a corner at high speed.

Caring for the Bicycle

Cleaning the Bicycle

Your bicycle should be cleaned often to keep it in good condition.

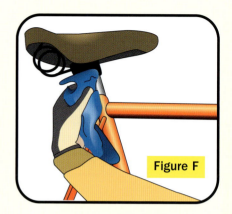
Figure F

- Dampen a cloth in a mixture of water and dish soap and clean the bicycle all over.
- Dry the bicycle with a soft cloth (Figure F).
- Use car or furniture wax to make your bicycle shine.

Preventing Rust

Follow these instructions to stop your bicycle from rusting.

- Store your bicycle in a sheltered place.
- If you ride your bicycle in the rain, dry it off with a towel after your ride.
- Use an antirust spray after washing your bicycle.
- If you find a chip in the paint, cover it with touch-up paint.

Oiling the Bicycle

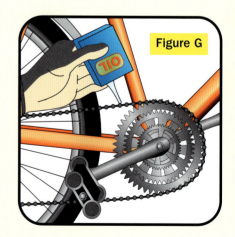
Figure G

- Oil the chain and cables regularly (Figure G).
- Wipe away excess oil. Over-oiling can cause dirt to stick to the chain.
- Do not oil the axle, crank, and gears. They have their own special grease.

Apply the Key Concepts

Key Concept 1 Machines use force to help people do work.

Activity

Think of four ways that you do work in sports. Create a concept web to show the different types of work. For each type of work, write whether the force moves, stops, or changes an object. Label the center of your concept web "Work and Sports."

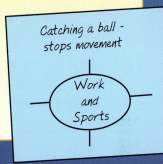

Catching a ball - stops movement

Work and Sports

Key Concept 2 There are six simple machines.

Activity

Think of two examples of simple machines found in sports. Draw these machines. Then label the parts that make them simple machines.

Arrow (wedge)

sloping surface

Key Concept 3 Compound machines use two or more simple machines operating together.

Activity

Draw two compound machines found in sports. Then label the different simple machines found within them. One has been started for you on the right.

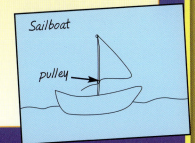

Sailboat

pulley

Write Your Own User Manual

You have read the user manual for the bicycle. Now you can think of a different machine that is used in sports and write a user manual for it.

1. Study the Model

Look back at the user manual on pages 23–26. What information is presented under each section? How do bulleted lists make the information easy to find and read? How do diagrams help you understand the information in the user manual?

2. Choose a Machine

Think of a machine that is used in sports. Draw the design of your machine. Make notes on what job the machine does and how the machine operates. Think of any safety precautions users will need to be told about.

User Manual

◆ Present the information in bulleted lists.

◆ Use diagrams to support the text.

◆ Break the information into easy-to-find sections.

◆ Include important safety precautions.

3. Write a User Manual

Use subheads that are similar to the ones in the bicycle user manual to write a user manual for your machine. Present the important information clearly in bulleted lists.

4. Draw Diagrams

Draw a diagram and label the different parts of your machine. Label all the parts that you refer to in the text. Then draw smaller diagrams to help illustrate the information in your bulleted lists.

Safety Precautions

- Wear a helmet.
- Wear knee and elbow pads.
- Check the wheels before using the machine.

5. Read over Your Work

Read over your user manual, correcting any spelling mistakes or punctuation errors. Make sure your user manual is easy to understand. Are your instructions for use easy to follow? Have you listed all the safety precautions? Did you describe how to care for the machine? Do your diagrams clearly illustrate the text? Is there any other information the user of your machine might need to know?

Present Your Machine

Now that you have chosen a machine and written a user manual for it, you can present the machine to the rest of the class.

How to Present Your Machine

1. Copy your labeled diagram onto an overhead transparency.
Draw the diagram clearly so you can show the different parts of your machine to the class.

2. Explain your machine to the class.
Take turns presenting your machines. Show the class the different parts of your machine on the overhead projector. Explain to the class what the machine is used for and how the machine works.

3. Explain the safety precautions.
It is important to follow the safety precautions carefully when you use any machine. Tell the class of any possible dangers with using your machine. Explain how to use the machine in the safest way possible.

4. Show the class how to care for the machine.
Tell the class how to clean, store, and care for the parts of your machine to keep it in the best working order.

Glossary

compound machines – machines that are made up of more than one simple machine

force – something that moves, changes, or stops an object

fulcrum – the fixed point on which a lever turns or swivels

gears – toothed wheels that work together to change the speed and/or direction of each other to cause movement

inclined plane – a slanted surface that is higher at one end than the other; also called a ramp

lever – a straight bar or rod that rotates about a fixed place

load – an object that a simple machine moves, stops, or changes

machines – tools or other devices that help people do work

pulley – a grooved wheel and rope system, used to move loads

screw – a pole with a ridge called a thread that spirals around it

simple machines – devices that change how forces act

thread – a sloped ridge that wraps around the pole of a screw

wedge – an object with one or more sloping sides that may end in a sharp edge or point

wheel and axle – a wheel joined to a pole or rod

work – the result of force moving, stopping, or changing an object

Index